Love's, Labour's, Lost

David Supper

Cyberwit.net
HIG 45 Kaushambi Kunj, Kalindipuram
Allahabad - 211011 (U.P.) India
http://www.cyberwit.net
Tel: +(91) 9415091004 +(91) (532) 2552257
E-mail: info@cyberwit.net

Introduction

David Supper has written an excellent collection of poems on love; a collection with the apt title "Love's, Labour's, Lost". He starts appropriately with the passion of love and lust, then moves into the labour involved with love, and finally onto the pain of lost love. David's style is clear and direct. It is almost conversational, drawing the reader into these themes of love. His poetry varies between strict rhythm and rhyme and a stream of consciousness flow.

The first section, devoted to the passion of love, opens up to the reader the wider scope of love, from a first kiss and being in heaven to the humorous modern method of dating online. David delves into the wide range of human emotions involved in love, magic, adventure, fear, delight and mystery. Often David includes descriptions of nature in his verses. The natural wedded to the emotions of love heightens the impact of love. In "Bluebells" he writes of lying on a carpet of bluebells; Where I held your hand and kissed your breast / And you clung to me as the bluebells fell, crushed by love." The second section goes deeply into the labour that love can bring. His poems here involve guilt, betrayal, failure, blame and pain. As Fickle Love describes; "A love's not love without the pain…" Yet love's labour is always worth it. As David writes with longing in "Just because"; "You do not have to love me just because I love you, but I pray that you might."

The last section speaks to love lost. In "fall" David writes "you fooled me, idiot that I was, to think you too could love me". He is honest with his emotions and thoughts, laying blame often on himself. His deep feelings and clear reflection do not shy away from difficult thoughts related to losing love including rejection and despair.

David has covered the scope of love in a beautifully lyric way. (His verse reminds me of that famous Biblical quote "love, faith and hope abide, these three, and the greatest of these is love.") Indeed the journey of love involves every bit of us. May the "wildness" in our hearts that David speaks of never subside.

Ralph Leavitt
Arch Deacon (Rtd.)
Diocese of Montreal, Canada

Foreword

In this collection of poems, my second, I hope that the reader will see these words as reflecting a journey, both good and bad – which is why I have divided them into three sections - as I searched for a one true love. It has at times seemed to be an elusive goal but I am happy to report that my search has been successful and I have included a few of the poems I have written celebrating a successful conclusion.

I have made many mistakes, some of which I am not proud, but hey! that's life.

I trust I have learnt many lessons, some of which you may find in these poems.

David Supper
July 2020

Contents

Love's

Bluebells

Whatever happened to those bluebells
Which carpeted the woodlands of south Oxfordshire?
Do you remember picking great armfuls, their lower stems
Gleaming in the sunlight like swords of fallen soldiers
Pointing skyward in heavenly despair?
And carrying them back in triumph to the car,
Only to see them wilt before we arrived home?

I took you into those woods and lay you down blue-carpeted,
And we watched the sunlight dance upon the ringing bells
As they strived to touch the stratosphere,
Mixing blue with blue, before a canopy of green shuts out the light;
And the wind blew warmly through the yellow of your hair.
I grew to love those woods where I first made love to you,
Where I held your hand and kissed your breast
And you clung to me as the bluebells fell, crushed by love.

Each year at April-time I return to breathe their scent, and in the heady
Atmosphere as I inhale the blue, I sometimes catch the smell of you
As your echo slips between the trunks and disappears.

Dating

Carol and Maggie, Patricia and Dee,
Sharon and Jackie, Ann and Val'rie,
Your hopes and your dreams you send them to me
Over the airwaves — elec-tron-ically

This mail and that mail, which male you see,
Depends on a whim eventually,
In this day and age it is likely to be
Anyone's guess — un-fortu-nately.

I wonder and wait for the picture to see,
For no matter how nice and gentle you be,
For us the outside is always the key
The decision is made — pic-tori-ally.

Emma and Katie, Ruth and Marj'rie,
I hope you'll not wait forever to see
A picture like Robbie, for he is not me
The truth you won't like — ac-tu-ally.

Knee Embrace

Under the restaurant table,
Your foot slips shoe
And wriggling toes
Inch upwards to my knee.
Your smile, fixed, intent,
As we wave away the waiter
And dessert.
Or side by side in the Playhouse,
Your hand beneath our coats
Gently stroking me hard,
A sudden squeeze, I gasp —
A merciless smile on your face
And my fingers are caught stockinged,
In the crease between calf and thigh.
Or homeward bound on the train,
Our knees chafe quite deliberately
In certain expectation
Of delights to come.

child of the night

when you lean forward
your face is in shadow
your hand reaches
out and the rings
on your fingers
glitter brightly
like stars in the night
your hand gently turns
revealing the palm
pale in the light
ringed by a moonstone

supple and suppliant
the long index finger
crowned by an arrowhead
the colour of blood
crooks like a shepherd
drawing me to you
narrowing the distance
between hate and love
I follow you meekly
into the shadows
away from the light

Just Because …

You do not have to love me
just because
you are all the women
I have ever wanted;
just because …
I have never felt so at ease
until I met you,
or so excited,
or so proud;
just because …
when we made love
I was so heroic,
so indomitable,
so powerful;
just because …
I take delight in you,
worship you,
want you,
ache for you.
You do not have to love me
just because I love you,
but I pray that you might.

A Perfect Present

All that you gave to me of you
I took and greedily wanted more.
Your touch, the smell of your hair
when I buried my face in your nape.
The way your body clung to mine
when we embraced, your softness,
the eagerness of your lips
when we kissed,
the thrust of your tongue.
This was the present you gave to me -
I could not have asked for more.

When you left you stole
my heart, and took
much more than you gave;
you were liquid, colourless,
and my blood flows like water.

Sonnet 5

You can be a pain in the backside sometimes,
especially when you have had a drink or two —
white wine disagrees with you, and always gives
a headache the next day, waving your hand
using a sign language, I give you Ibuprofen.
I love seeing your face screwed up in childish fury
suddenly change, the lines of your anger remain,
traced on your face around your eyes, your forehead.
Mostly I love you curled up on the sofa
your body swallowed by cushions, your head
marooned in a red moquette sea. When you smile,
anger like chaff, blows away in the wind;
the room glows with light and I remember, flushed
with youth, another room when you gave yourself to me.

The Lost Cause

I looked for love
But couldn't find it,
Thought I saw it
On another plate,
But was fooled
And used for comfort;
Blind I did not see
How much I needed,
Or how great
The pain would be
When I was discarded.
Foolishly I looked again
Not once or twice
But thrice I fell,
Into a trap
Of my own making.

I did not learn
From my mistakes,
And truth to tell
Would do it all again
For a chance to find
That love to satisfy
My yearning,
Fill the emptiness
I feel and cast away
My burden;
So I can sleep
And then awake

Refreshed to spend
The remainder of my days
With you, in harmony
And peace, without dissent,
Knowing I have found love.

M

I never thought of you being dead.
That summer picking nectarines
in your oversized glasshouse,
nervous fumblings as we sat watching
the light fade to dusk and then to night.
Your long legs wrapped around my body,
Let's be naughty you whispered
leading me to the bedroom.
I did not know what to expect —
you were hot inside
and I was too old to be a virgin.
We made love twice that night
and I lay in your arms without dreaming.

I saw you once more before you died,
still as beautiful and elegant
but you had lost interest in making love.
All that sweat and body fluids, the smells
and mess no longer interests me
you said, but I noticed you still
rubbed your leg against mine.
Your eyes gleamed in the lamplight,
the pearl at your throat glowed
in memory of our passion long ago.
I heard later the glasshouse was destroyed
in a winter storm and, where we
once lay, stands a block of flats.

You Whose Beauty

You whose beauty does compare
With all that nature has to offer,
You whose lips I long to kiss
And taste the honey in your mouth,
You whose slender body I yearn to touch
And feel the softness of your skin,
You whose perfume draws me ever closer
And tempts me to commit a sin.

Yet you are distant, set aside by age,
Two generations silences my tongue,
Still I ache to feel you by my side,
Your hands exploring all I have to give,
Your lips in supplication to the Gods
As you drink the nectar of my prayers.

Awakening

It is moribund to talk of weather,
the wind blows across frontiers
driving warm or cold fronts,
not waiting for passport control
or immigration. It lurks in ditches,
behind walls and under trees,
as well as in the upper air, where
we feel it caressing our faces.

Rain or no rain, we shelter our
inner thoughts, remembering
from our past, moments of happiness
or embarrassment, smells like
mown grass and summer rain.
I remember the first kiss, the wetness,
the warmth, tongues sliding together,
heart beating, a hardness in the groin.

Then running home with water
streaming down my face, not caring
about the gusting wind or the thunder,
for I had been in heaven; wrapped
in a blanket, my senses on fire,
oblivious of the outside world,
That night I made love to the pillow -
As if it were you.

Forbidden Fruit

I see your hair hang heavily
and smell your earthy scent
the ripeness of your cheeks
with a rosy blush of red
your ruby lips are tempting
the juice inside is sweet
the whiteness of my teeth
to bite and crush your skin
and still I want to taste
forbidden pleasures' lust
feel the warmth inside
and eat the pip within

I am ...

I am blue on a summer's day,
I am the sun shining wanly through clouds,
I am rain dripping in gutters,
I am wind chasing leaves from the trees,
I am a staircase waiting for footsteps,
I am thin and cannot be seen;
I am the dark seeking a light,
I move in the air and float above —
I am a wraith seeking my love.

Ignis fatuus

Meet me in the fields,
the water meadows with the long grass
where we used to meet when we were in love,
you remember, when the light sparkled in your eyes
while we undressed, and we dug our toes into the soft loam,
then watched the swans sail serenely by, white tails wagging.

Nothing has happened right since those dream-like days,
you leave me all over again and again, like a melody
that hangs on the wind, like birdsong in Spring,
you are not real anymore; now I am uncertain
if you were a fallen angel, or something
more wicked in my thoughts.

On the floor, your ballet clothes screwed up
with my pyjamas, abandoned, empty. I feel your hand
slither on my naked skin, you draw in my smell,
male you say, we share the moment as your head nestles
in that place below my chin, where nothing is required — but
silence.

Magic Moments

We stopped the car in an RSPB car park;
a broad track, several metres above the marsh,
swept out to the invisible sea beyond the dunes.

Red and orange quad bikes were being off-loaded
by men in knitted uniforms, who seemed in no hurry,
as they chatted, fiddled and smoked Marlboros.

The dog raced ahead as the full force of the wind
drove us to find shelter, gulls shrieked from above
mocking our faint hearts, goading us onwards.

We never reached the sea, but in the distance
stood the pier, marooned in a sea of sand,
we stand awkwardly, like teenagers on a first date.

That night we explore each other's bodies,
our kisses, wild and passionate, taken greedily,
our mouths starved of comfort for so long.

In days where days can be counted and summer
slips into autumn, I enter you … in the stillness that follows,
we lie in shocked disbelief, hand in hand — stargazing.

Under Cabbage-green Skies

A slight trace of fear is felt as wind tears through trees,
howls over chimneys like a lone animal in pain,
rain lashes at the windows like hardened peas on a drum.
Crushed leaves slowly compost, lie thickly on pavements,
a weak sun casts thin shadows in mockery of other seasons.

Your thin arms grip tightly as if your life depended on holding me,
love binds us together, your face a pale yellow circle in the dim light.
I murmur soothing words and the bed, like a raft, is blown
this way and that — until it noses, settles, into a soft mud-bank
and beneath a weeping willow we drift uneasily into sleep.

Clarice

I see you standing with your friends,
Your blonde hair shining in the light,
Your youth brings colour to your cheeks
Your laughter sings a song to me;
The sparkle in your eyes, your energy
Is more precious than a diamond,
More valuable than all the gold
In the mask of Tutankhamun.

Your smile when you gave it to me,
Warmed the icicles inside my heart,
And made me want to jump for joy,
Shout out loud and ring the bells
To let the whole world know
About that look that made me glow.

For Bryony

When first we met and you served boiled chicken
then hovered around like an anxious waiter,
I soon realised there we were, in the middle of nowhere,
fumbling with strings of life in the dark.

It didn't take long to fall in love,
although when it came, it was quite a surprise;
I looked into your eyes and I could see
your mouth curl inwardly in a secretive smile,

your eyes laughed, even mocked
but I knew it was intended only for me.
I knelt at your feet, a fine kind of man,
a man who makes jam, kissing your hands.

We shouldn't have met, wires got crossed
and for once happenstance happened;
you fell for my humour, but I fell for your
wonky good looks under glycerine skies.

Labour's

On Writing a Difficult Letter

Dear John … That's how all these letters are begun
Or in my case that should be now — dear Jane ……
I think of all the girls I've known and how it all began —
A look of shy embarrassment and then a smile,
Followed by a faltering word or two until the conversation flows
And an accidental touch, as we stand closer, closer — kiss and, aah
That's easy — but ending is more difficult
And, when you know it's over, what's to do?
A face-to-face discussion, it is the honest way
For heroes and those men of steel but not, I fear, for I —
For I am just a mortal, a coward in my heart
And so I take this easy way of writing in a letter:
Dear Jane …
I've had enough of all your lies, deceiving little baggage!
It's over, finished — now fuck off! Love, David.
There, that's done, succinct and to the point
I think I've made it very clear, I think she'll get the message.

Eyes Wide Open

Who would or could not know
or understand how deep
the wounds of words, or still
the blinding, numbing despair
of indifference to a lover;
causing such a torrent,
a gushing stream,
unacceptable realisation
that it's over, ended, finished.
Defeated.
Still hope lives on
a dying ember, true,
waiting for the breath of love
to glow, shine brightly,
burst forth from red into
yellow/orange glory, flickering,
burning and bursting the heart
until, with eyes blinded and bleeding
love melts and slips away.
Forever.

In My Dreams

In my dreams you are there
waiting for me with open arms
and a smile upon your face

you wipe away the tears on mine
and hold me to your breast
you stroke my hair and kiss my lips

and say 'we've been apart so long
now come my love and stay with me
we'll be together from now on

I'll ease your pain and you'll be mine
from now until the end of time'
I reach out to hold you close

and feel your warmth beside me
but all is air as I wake alone
and now the pain returns

all I want and all I need
I find within my dreams
so now I'll sleep, no more to wake

and share my life with the one I lost,
though only in my dreams

The Photograph

There you are, smiling at me
pleased as punch,
and so you should be —
we laid on the grass
in the sun,
and you were.
I lean closer,
inches from the surface
you seem so real,
three-dimensional,
I almost smell your perfume.
Closer, my eyes deceive me
I feel giddy:
and then we are kissing
madly; passionately;
your tongue in my mouth;
heart pounds
head spins
like we had never parted,
I could not get enough.
Closer, I tried to catch a breath,
I could not see you
or feel you;
choking I spat out
the lump of soggy paper,
that was your photograph.

Hope

Deep along the hedgerow
where blackbirds sing their song,
where yellowhammers perch,
and tits both great and blue
dart in and out to build their nests,
and where the song thrush
plays a tune before the day's begun.
In that denseness of the border
where columbine weaves her way,
with a tantara of trumpets
opening every day,
there is sometimes found
a gap or chink where light,
comes streaming through
to give a partial view
of the fields that lie beyond,
where a skylark may be heard
singing at the sun.
Watch her eagerness for flight
while we stand remote,
rooted to the ground.

That day I first met you
first felt the torment of your touch,
the taste of all you offered
when you opened up to me,
how I soared and swallowed
and drunk with all that honey,
we rode the air together

dancing with the wind,
high above those fields
until it seemed I was that lark.
I stretched, ruffled feathers
and arched my neck to see
you so perfect and impossible …
then the moment passed and
every hope that I had dreamed
came crashing down like
shattered shards of glass,
for you swept towards your nest
without a backward glance —
and I remain, waiting for you
to honour your promises.

You Leave Me Nowhere

The turmoil deep inside invades my thoughts
when I am left alone, a stranger in my mind
walks with slow, dark steps, ready to run
and hide, avoiding the slightest human touch.

I find no shield can protect me from the eyes
of those who wander in and out of daily life,
not knowing if they know what I feel, that I am
burning inside, seeing secretly what I value most.

In whom can I now confide? The rivers, forests
even the air itself that witness the kind of life
that I am forced to follow, concealed from all,

cannot arm me or strengthen my resolve against
the power of Love, who finds and whispers to me
in wild, inaccessible places — far from reality.

Sonnet 6

Half listening, half there listening to me, love,
I hear the thuds of your heart; you, deep in thought
on the momentous decision we have just made.
This time you have not changed your mind;
steadfastly anchored, you make plans for the future
standing amidst drawings, designs bricked up in
architectural follies, you plough on — demented.
Even nature falls beneath your spells, trees felled.
Seated at your desk in the gathering gloom
you are buoyant, unagitated, you don't get ill,
but last week you said you wept with frustration:
I tried to feel your pain but we don't communicate,
I'm listening of course, standing ill-at-ease and
waiting for you to open the gates of affection.

The Interior (after Degas)

Crushed, her face hidden with shame
she kneels, her torn chemise reveals
pale skin, delicate, defenceless.

He stands against the door
hirsute, red-faced and angry,
his shadow darkly on the wall.

The virgin bed waits primly
to be scarred and stained blood-red;
in all innocence of tenderness

lust replaces love, hardens hearts.
No hero or gallant will knock upon the door,
this night her fate, her future is secured.

In grace she kneels to pray, fearing to hope
against the vanity of a man, the surging rush
that pulls her apart, gorged and broken.

The State of Clay

I've waited for you long enough, each time we meet
I always ask 'has your divorce come through at last?'
You always answer with a laugh 'it's you that left, not me.'
You married and despite my pleas moved to some
Godforsaken village, that can't make up its mind
between a bastion of England or Cornish independence.

Next time you come to see your Mother I will have left,
sold up and moved away from here. No more drinks in
local pubs or fiery curries or doggy bags. I won't hear
the stories of your cats' misdeeds or how you've made
a life so far away (from me), the allotment and the state
of clay, the rainfall and how your vegetables have grown.

I will not suffer when you tell of others you have seen,
or the deluded slob – your ex, who fondly dreams,
through a whisky haze, that you and he will re-unite
in some ghastly parody of wedded bliss, forgetting
how he made the hell that you endured. Nor will I ever
have to ask again how you survive without my love.

I always thought that somehow, you and I would be
together, first as lovers, then as friends and finally
entwined as man and wife. I see now that was a foolish
dream, full of fancies and delusions, how could I be
so blind to mistake your kisses, and the way you held
me so your body clung to mine in close embrace, for love.

When I told you, in a text, that I was going, your reaction
was a loss of words, or so you said, although later you were
'devastated' and said that I was going far too far away,
too far for us to see each other. What you do not understand
is that after all this time I have had enough of being teased,
dangled on a string and wrapped around your little finger.

Finally I have woken up, seen that my future is not with you,
I have to dull the pain and close the wound of separation,
a final wrench, an elastoplast sharp rip and pulled away
from new-formed skin, which I have sewn together, layered
to protect my heart, before I go. I don't know if we'll meet
again, but my regret is that you never once asked me to stay.

Cooking up an Argument

You put a pizza in the oven overloaded with mushrooms,
onions and red peppers, sprinkled with pine nuts, raisins,
tails of anchovies, dressed with olive oil and black pepper.
Slamming the oven door you said you didn't know Harrogate,
and what would we do there for three days (and nights), 'I need
entertainment,' you insisted, 'I don't want to sit in an hotel room.'
You were in a strop and wouldn't listen to reason,
'Google the bloody place', I snapped back.

We argue a lot these days, you draw back when I touch,
kisses are rare, I am grateful we still share the same bed
but sex is a distant memory. I slipped and fell on the stairs
tearing ligaments in the ankle. Now Harrogate is cancelled
and you screw your face in disappointment,
I thought you hated the place — but maybe you just wanted to argue.

Bookcases

We argued about bookcases but that was just an excuse,
a reason to argue and these days we don't need reasons.
The argument grew to include lampstands, your furniture,
my furniture. Then there were the buses, passing the door
every ten minutes, what can I do about buses? Suddenly
I'm blamed for everything that's wrong and you burst
into tears, when that doesn't work you start shouting
and screaming and swearing. I'm always in the wrong.

What happened to us? You sit on your fragile chair
with your sad thoughts, your blonde hair showing grey,
and I want to kiss away your sorrows, your sadness –
but somehow I can't reach you. The nape of your neck
says kiss me, rescue me from this abyss, you promised:
all I can think of is to ask for forgiveness, not knowing why.

The Card

Today I sent her my last card
her indifference to me I have borne
the pain she inflicted deep despair
loneliness when she said goodbye
I kept my word
my part of the bargain she promised
it would not be long my lover
my muse consumed with desire
I burned felt foolish I was weak
without peace I could not rest
she was a gazelle easily startled
I knew she would never return
years passed passion-like fire
dies without fuel but my resolve
lacks strength I try to let go
I sought contentment I remember
her needs in fields beneath trees
on riverbanks under hedgerows
how much she gave to me
and how lost I was drowning
in her neglect

inside the card I wrote a note
she would never read poured my pain
into every word each comma stop
and semicolon absorbed the anguish
but left the memories intact

Fickle Love

And here am I left all alone
To ponder on my poetry,
To seek a muse who'll give me fire,
The heat of which I choose to use
To write of love which passed me by,
Left me alone to ponder on
And seek the reasons why.

A lover's scorn is hard to bear
When passion rules the heart,
I bend my knee to plead my case,
And if that fails put pen to paper
Write a letter full of prose,
A rhyme or two, a curlicue
To save a love I dare not lose.

And if I fail to move her heart,
I let her see a teardrop fall
Onto my beardless cheek,
A love's not love without the pain
Of reconciliation's beauty,
And so we lie as lovers do
Intertwined for Cupid's duty.

When my ardour's sated,
The fire of love put out
Quenched in her cool hand,
I turn my thoughts to other loves
Those that turned me down,
For I have sworn to make them sweat
And answer me without a sound.

And then in years to come
When I look back and count the cost
That love has meant to me,
I'll have the satisfaction
That none has passed me by,
All those ladies I have bedded
Not one has made me cry.

Like a fish

Like a fish on a line
You keep me dangling there,
Unrequited love
Is the hardest love to bear.

A lobster in the pot
Is worth two in the sea,
Isn't it possible
For you to love me?

Like a fish on a line
You have me hooked,
I swallowed the bait
And now I am fucked.

When the tide turns
Then you'll be sorry,
I'll turn my back
And won't have to worry.

Like a fish on a line
I wriggled and danced,
To the tune that you play
To keep me entranced.

You'll see what a catch
You let slip away,
Then you'll regret it
Day after day.

Going Back

I've tried going back to where I used to live:
the house is the same, the front door a different colour,
the stained glass window that I found
in the back streets of Bradford, still there in the porch,
the front garden unkempt, neglected, tired.

I lived in this house for fifteen years, as I searched for …
… what? Love? Security, comfort, peace of mind?
I tried going back to a half-remembered dalliance
from my youth, she was much older than I expected,
lined, worn with experience, worn out emotionally.

The thought that it might be made to work
was in both our minds. I didn't recognise the weakness,
the fatal flaws that her character had absorbed,
or was it that I never really knew her, lived only in a dream
of what she was, what I made her, made me believe.

I threw caution to the wind, jumped in without a parachute,
loved her with a passion, mistook lust for requited love.
How wrong I was, she grew to hate me,
hate me for not being a perfect replacement,
to excise betrayal, become a father to a flawed family.

I failed her, and at the same time I failed myself,
the grail I sought seems beyond reach, beyond the setting sun.
I have nothing to do but fall, freefall as if in a dream:
where you hold on tight to yourself, screw your eyes closed,
hope for soft landings, hope to wake up.

Dreams 1

Just this morning,
in that delightful place
between half asleep and half awake,
I thought I felt your hand upon my face.

This evening
just before I fell asleep,
I thought I heard you call my name
and felt your lips upon my cheek.

When first we meet
it does not matter how we feel,
only pray that love survives
and broken hearts can heal.

Sometimes

Sometimes words are useless,
sometimes there is nothing more to say,
sometimes just feeling is the only way,
sometimes even tears are not enough,
sometimes silence can be rough,
sometimes a touch can really please,
but sometimes a hug can mean …
… so much more than all of these.

The Bed

Crumpled duvet carelessly thrown back,
a counterpane, edges drip with plastic beads,
cold green sheets, a fight over pillows,
a memory of shared beds, shared times.
I am out of love with sex, a firm snake
that dove into wet burrows, try to remember –
was it all worthwhile, the fire, the passion?

Now I sleep alone, or spend the night
with the radio, fight tears, there is no warmth
by my side, a flat plain instead of rolling hills;
night cramps grab at my legs instead of you,
I turn and slurp tepid water from a Coke glass,
swallow a rainbow collection of pills.
In the morning race for the bathroom,

I see you, looking prettier then ever.

In the car ...

… we drove on, icily,
I could hear the words
you hadn't said:
blaming me
for another disaster.

You never take me out
you had said earlier,
and, in a moment
of weakness, almost love,
I had replied, 'Well,
why don't you come tonight?'
From the moment we entered the room
I knew it had been a mistake.
You complained about the wine,
the position of your chair,
the people around you,
most of whom I didn't know,
you wanted to leave before the end
and grumbled
when I said I wanted to stay.
You insisted on a mince pie
and then refused to pay —
I seem to pay for everything
these days.
You wanted to talk
to strangers before we left
and take another's coat.
You were almost angry

when we stumbled out
into the night air.

I look across
at your profile,
which has sagged
since last week,
at the bead of sweat
on your upper lip
and wonder
what I still see in you.

At the end

I gave you ten years
of my life:
I tried everything
to make you happy,
to compensate
for a failed marriage
and children
damaged
by your ex,
until now —
I am sick
of trying

You never loved me,
I fooled myself,
you took
but gave little back;
blood thicker than water
holds you
to the past,
your present
or future
is of little consequence

You do not want to be a nursemaid,
although I am not an invalid
your patience is wearing thin,
how can we remain friends
when you are tearing my heart apart?

I will remember you,
cutting your toenails,
clippings falling
like diamonds,
on the lounge floor.

Lost

Despair

I lie under the southern sun,
the sickly-sweet scent of jasmine
fills the air, I am suffocating.
Snake-like you move against me,
your dark hair piercing my skin.
I am naked — and at your mercy;
you swallow me whole,
swallow my world
from the inside out.

You switched off the light
and turned on my darkness.

Amor furor brevis est

Across a Tuscan field under an Umbrian sky
Blue-remembered hills of yesterdays gone by,
Tall cypritic columns of deep viridian green
Evoke memories of you and what might have been;

Terracotta walls warm in the yellow sun
Traced with shadows when the day is done.
Hand in hand we walked as lovers down the hill
And left the landscape to the night, silent, still.

Through the inner courtyard, climbed the marble stair
Opened up the window, gave ourselves some air,
Hot and sticky, barely touching, we lay upon the bed
Until the fury that was ours could not be gainsaid.

I woke exhausted in the morning my hand between your thigh
You moved a little closer and whispered with a sigh,
'Remember me this moment, this perfect moment now'
And I knew that it was over and I could not ask you how.

I saw make-up on your face and a strange look in your eye
I did not have the courage or the strength to ask you why.
Crumpled bed clothes on the floor lay like Tracy at the Tate
Stained and soiled as are lilies, abandoned to their fate.

Dreams 2

I dream of a wildness in my heart,
Wildness where the waters meet;
I see the wilderness of love
Desert me in my hour of need.

In my dreams there is another way,
Where I am king and all is peace;
I see how different life can be
When one is two, in equal quantity.

I wonder what you're thinking now?
If your skin is still as smooth,
The way you moved and held your head,

Sends me into raptures even now.
You never knew how much I loved,
Nor guessed the pain you caused.

For MB

Your night in the days of our youth
was warm and moist
and lit by a lemon moon,
scudding behind ragged clouds
to the sound of the wind
and a rustle of dead leaves.
Blonde upon blonde
tumbling down full-waisted,
splitting and darting,
framing your pale face.
Hand in hand I led you
hope following prayer,
feeling and touching
a curve here, a softness there;
chased and a chaste kiss
was my reward.
In my days of approaching old age
when those nights come again,
I think of you,
the shine of your hair,
the moon in your eye —
and I ache with sadness and despair.

On a Journey from Lancashire to the M1

Driven and grey came the rolling clouds,
grey upon grey streaked wet with rain,
touching the moorland with a sigh,
splashing the windscreen in the fading light.

Oncoming lights starburst in my eyes,
failing to warm the coldness inside;
the hills disappear in a blur to the sky
and the beat of the day turns into the night.

Nights are the worst, they remind me of you,
when you stole to my arms and pulled me inside
to make love as you wanted, with never a thought

that what we were doing would alter a life.
When you walked away and left me alone
in rolled the clouds, drenching my heart.

Nothing

That first betrayal, when I stood in the doorway
watching you two clinging together, inseparable,
like Siamese twins. I was only sixteen, the shock
was too much to bear. We had spent every day,
the whole holiday, nearly two weeks, in each
other's company, avoiding inquisitive parents,
avoiding intercourse – but not much else.

You were my first real girlfriend, torn away,
shredded like so much waste paper, binned,
discarded. I felt my face redden, the prickling
of skin, embarrassed, not knowing what to say
I stood rooted to the spot, while he, noticing
my presence, whispered to you and laughed
softly: you looked at me and I felt like nothing.

When the summer was over, you sent me a letter
explaining your guilt, your treason, your reasons;
but I could only see you as ivy, entwined on a tree,
clinging, as I changed from a boy to a man —
that summer, when you danced for me
to a forty-five played on an old Dansette:
it was only make-believe, sang Conway Twitty.

Absence

When here, you are almost annoying:
slippers scattered in the hall, on stairs,
like confetti in a graveyard.

You leave half-filled coffee cups
congealing in unexpected places;
I think how we have spent our lives

these last eight years.

Yet your presence is, strangely comforting —
that faint waft of perfume, body lotions,
skin creams, catches me in unguarded moments,

fills the house like bunches of flowers
that you stuff in every room, dried petals
curling, staining window ledges and floors.

Now you have gone
I am broken,
abandoned like an empty chair.

The Empty Chair

She sat patiently by the fireside,
only her hands moving as she sewed.

The light flickered on her face,
the flames glistened in her eyes.

Her gaze focused on the chair where he always sat,
the cushion dimpled with the shape of his bottom.

She would trace the shape with her hand,
— always without touching.

Sadly she put her work to one side
and plunged her hands deep into the fire.

Couples

I saw her again today, seated on the grass
outside The Swan, the sun backlit her hair,
bleached-blonde, corn-cob yellow.

She turned her head and I saw a pony tail,
this was a younger, much younger former self,
imprinted in my memory, like her dazzling smile.

How many times do I see her now?
Always in couples as I sit alone, on my own;
she walks with others, lovers, straw-haired children.

Entwined amongst the flowers I see her,
I wait for a turn of her head, to see her face,
and I, with a sigh, watch couples go by.

The Broad Way

I should have known
when you wouldn't tell me your address,
that this thing was never going to happen.

Let's be honest,
you did not trust me
and without trust there was no chance.
We both wanted something different:
with me it was sex or love
or both, I don't know anymore.

Only you knew what you wanted,
I could not fathom you out,
you blew hot and cold
like a will o' the wisp.

At the end
you did not return my calls,
so I retreated into dreams
where you were so soft, unformed,
and there were no words
to wrestle with,
or to tell lies.

The Loser

It was a bad day for Peter,
the last day as one half of a couple;
she left him, moved into the spare room —
shaken, he reacted badly.

Everything changed, like when snow falls
blanketing the streets,
thickening the garden,
black footsteps pockmark the surface.

Already he missed her,
she had plucked his feathers,
skin all puckered, exposed, stripped bare,
vulnerable, lost and alone.

He was caught in a trap,
reality drifted slowly away,
in his eyes a look of great loss,
like he had slipped into another body.

It was not his skin,
yet he wrapped it around him
like a cloak of invisibility:
he thinks 'in time, I'll see clearly again'.

This House

This house that I am now leaving
was meant to be forever,
it was chosen with love in mind,

decorated by Laura Ashley,
subtle colours that blended
from room to room,

feature papers on just one wall.
This was a house you could sleep in,
feel the pride of belonging,

owning, nurturing, a house
(and a garden) to potter in,
it was a comfortable house.

This house that I am now leaving
feels empty, with boxes of emotions
piled high in the halls,

hollow laughter mocks me
as I dismantle the lies,
take down the promises,

paint over the hopes,
watch the sun set,
rain glistens on roof tiles.

A last look at an old-fashioned house,
while a radio plays a familiar, sweet love song:
a house I should have kept, like a secret.

To forget her infidelity

She's leaving for another county,
way down south,
I'm burnt out trying to please,
suffering her sudden heated anger,
her ginger son who creeps round corners
listening, drooling, clawing her back to him.

I blame global warming,
traffic, double-decker buses on the road outside,
the morbidly obese, spontaneous combustion,
so far from the sea;
the gods are angry with me
and have unleashed their vengeful fire.

This is where I belong,
although I am afraid of being alone;
when grief comes
I'll keep nothing but her name,
engraved upon a stone
in the wasteland she has made my home.

fall

the sun sewn above the horizon
and clouds stitched around
into a scratched and patchwork sky —
a soft, yellow-filtered afternoon
threaded through undressed trees,

birds sing unheard melodies
and distant dog barks echo
unfledged, where mutilated
memories are singly drawn,
dredged up to keep me in my place;

I remember you, your tanned skin
below thick grey hair, iron-sided,
premature to belie your age —
you caught me in your trap,
no iron bars held me fast,

trapped, deluded, I self-harmed —
internalised the pain and the markings
long since bloodied and scarred,
there the light scattered, breaking,
breaking me, who simply loved you;

you fooled me, idiot that I was,
to think you too could love me

Grief

When it came they were on the island
sitting awkwardly side by side,
nothing was said, could be said,
the silence became unbearable,

she, still in her underclothes,
slipped into the water and swam
towards the weir, the last he saw
was her blonde hair shining

against the steel grey machinery,
the green water, before it plunged
with a rush, a roar to the lower level;
foaming, dancing without mercy.

In shock he took the boat, the oars,
rowed, water swirled from the blades
as he pulled against the current, calling her,
calling her name in his river of loss.

Lost Love

Does it end so soon
before it has begun
like chaff blowing in the wind
or ships that pass i' the night?
The nectar of your lips
will ne'er pass mine again,
the sweet taste of you
remains forbidden fruit
and I, despairingly, pass into
the mists of time — and
ghostlike, echo in the memories of your mind.

Tantric

When I think of you, I think of lovers,
valiant as in days of knights. I armed myself,
girded and strong, or so I thought,
for the battle of my hearts-ease.

Close, I heard you breathe me in and
as the very essence passed between us,
north and south our bodies pulled together,
we touched — I was yours and I worshipped you.

My eyes blinded with your sweet tears,
I raised the tri-colour, drank in your scent
dear jackanapes, and felt myself drowning.

The sweetness of your body … no match for
the bitterness of rejection; when it came I was
defenceless, against the wildness in my heart.

Carpe Diem

If I close my eyes
I can imagine you here,
lying beside me,
your hand resting on my thigh,
your head on my chest.

If I breathe in
I can smell your hair
and the dampness
on your skin,
a faint musty odour
I remember so well.

You stir sleepily,
I hear a sigh of content
leave your lips;
I crane my head
in an effort to see your face,
but you nuzzle my neck.

In the silence that follows
I become confused,
I'm thinking of you, of us,
wide-eyed I paw
the empty air by my side:
I am not awake.

Wound in a sheet, disorientated,
I could hear your voice:

I told you, I told you
But you wouldn't listen;
in my sleep I cried,
oh how I cried.

When my heart stops …

… or skips a beat
there is a moment of silence,
of unreality, as the world slows
its relentless pace;
a pause before an intake of breath —
but you are not there,
the emptiness of the sofa
dimpled where your bottom pressed.

In the dark recesses of my mind
where memory lurks unseen,
unwanted, yet there inevitably,
like day passing into night,
is a stillness that comes at last
like some small death,
monumental in its own way,
gnawing nagging, pulling me apart —

the rhythmic pounding of a lonely heart.

In this place

You stand on the garden path
at the top of the brick steps,
overlooking the lower lawn,
staring down at me;
your face set as in a mask.
I thought I knew you.

I looked up,
you had moved into the space
once occupied by the copper beech.
I waited for you to speak,
to tell me of your love.
How in this garden
everything was perfect.

The sunshine warm on my back
as I waited to hear of love —
but you did not speak.

In this silence the weather changed,
we are the victims of circumstance
our paths are widening.

This is how we end.